This is a **FLAME TREE NOTEBOOK**
Designed, published and © copyright 2014 Flame Tree Publishing Ltd
Based on an original image by Vector Ninja/Shutterstock.com

Wings of a Rose • ISBN 978-1-78361-144-7

FLAME TREE PUBLISHING LIMITED
Crabtree Hall, Crabtree Lane, London SW6 6TY, United Kingdom
www.flametreepublishing.com

All rights reserved. Printed in China